FULL CIRCLE

My Supernatural Healing from Stress to Wholeness

SHARON D. JONES

Copyright © 2025 Sharon D. Jones

All rights reserved. This publication may not be reproduced in any form without permission in writing from the publisher. Unauthorized reproduction of any part of this work is illegal and is punishable by law.

Scripture references are used with permission from Zondervan via Biblegateway.com

ISBN 978-1-950861-90-3

PRINTED IN THE UNITED STATES OF AMERICA

Wendell, North Carolina

DEDICATION

I dedicate this book to my husband, Kelvin Jones, my mother Naomi Baker, my sister Jakki Baker, and daughters Kayla Baker and Kaiya Baker. You have been with me through it all and I am SO GRATEFUL!

I also dedicate this book to anyone who believes in miracles and those who need miracles.

ACKNOWLEDGEMENTS

Most of all, I would like to thank my Lord and Savior Jesus Christ who brought me through such a challenging time and spoke to me about writing this book since 2017. I have been dedicated to pursuing this vision, believing it will impact the lives of many people.

As with everything I have done in my life, this book would not have been possible without the outpouring of love and support of many people. I would not be the person that I am today without the unconditional love of my mother, Naomi Baker. She has always been there for me, allowing me not to fall too far down, that I could not get back up.

My husband Kelvin Jones is my forever long-time love and committed father to our daughters. We have much history and our story is forever unfolding. I meekly await for the next supernatural to take place in our lives.

Jakki, my one and only sister, you have been with me through thick and thin, ups and downs. I couldn't imagine life without you. Your love, concern, and support mean EVERYTHING to me. Thank you for laboring with me!

My daughters Kayla and Kaiya, for being in the right place at the right time with maturity and strength. You are forever treasures in my heart! You continuously show me what unconditional love feels like. Thank you so much for being there for me!

Cousin/ Sister Val (my Ace), thank you for keeping me straight, pushing me forward, cheering me on, and listening to me in the early mornings and the late evenings. No matter the distance that separates us, you hold a special place in my heart; I will cherish and nurture our bond always.

I am forever grateful for my family and friends. Unfortunately, I cannot list you all. However, I must extend my heartfelt thanks to Pastor James T. Elam Jr. and his wife Sister Penny. Also, Minister Rhonda,

Barbara, Linda, Angie, Nanette and my prayer warriors. You have experienced, along with me, what gut-level, crying out to God and intercession for my total healing really means. Your faithfulness to God and prayers caused God's angels to work on my behalf.

Bon Secours DePaul Hospital: I also want to thank Dr. John R. Baker MD, PH.D, one of the top acknowledged Neuroendovascular interventionist in the country, and Dr. Crystal J. Baker-Wray, DNP, FNP-C, PMHNP-BC. Your care was phenomenal and exceptional. Your mannerisms and expert care put me at ease and helped me to keep the faith and confidence of knowing ALL WILL BE WELL. I am VERY WELL, and I want to express my heartfelt gratitude for your unwavering dedication and compassionate care.

Finally, I want to thank Coach Felicia Lucas, His Glory Creations Publishing LLC team and Armor of Hope Writing. Your patience and expertise have been amazing.

Table of Contents

Introduction 1

Chapter 1 – Filling The Void 3

Chapter 2 – Stat... The Unexpected 9

Chapter 3 – Recovery 23

Chapter 4 – New Life 35

About The Author 41

INTRODUCTION

Hey, Hey Now!

I have a story to tell---

This is a major opening to my book, where I hype you up more about what to look forward to reading my book.

We were made for MORE!

The purpose of this is not to boast about my healing nor marrying my forever husband.

Its purpose is to deal truthfully of where you are in life, know who God is to you and have a personal relationship with Him.

The doctors and nurses thought I was going to die.

They were most definitely wrong!

Let's start with me asking a question: Have you ever been in a situation not knowing whether you will live or die due to unforeseen circumstances and/or were life may be taking you?

It was my faith and knowing God loves me so much that resilience on the inside of me to live. Divine Healing that saved my life in 2016, was the miraculous.

I believe in this season God's people will be on display. Century of disbelief, stress and any form of depression will come to an end. However, yes things will happen in life that is totally out of your control but know there is a higher power to trust in, which is the spirit of God's son Jesus himself.

As you take a cruise through these chapters keep an open mind and spirit knowing that whatever you may be going through, miracles are in the atmosphere and God's love for you is more than you will ever imagine because of His Grace and Mercy.

Love,
Sharon

CHAPTER 1

FILLING THE VOID

I have been in the church all my life, growing in faith, and becoming a woman of order as I am today. One day, my faith was tried. I was a single mother of two girls, working a stressful full-time job, and attending college part-time. Last, but not least... I was an active member at my church, Dunamis Christian Center, as a prayer leader, altar worker and a part of the core team of the Single's ministry. As I did those things, I believed God would give me the desires of my heart, which was to be married someday. As I continued, I began to feel, Surely there is more to life than this. I began to feel stressed, short of patience, and ran down without an outlet. Again, I thought, there has to be more.

I began feeling a void...empty, lonely, and isolated. I prayed, "Lord, please send me someone that I can just hang out with...have dinner, walks on the beach, or just have talks." Before I knew it, God had answered my prayer by showing me a friend who I called my best friend. This was someone I had known for several years. He was always there but only for a season. It was a long time since I felt good! However, as we began spending time getting to know one another, I thought, maybe he could be more than my best friend. Then, reality set in... He is married.

Whether his marriage was not all he wanted it to be, the fact remained the same...he was married. Our friendship was the best. We talked about a lot of things and on many different levels, from the word of God, our children, and more. The more we talked and spent time together, we grew closer and closer spiritually, emotionally, and physically. In my mind (boy how the mind can play tricks on you), I thought it was nothing wrong with having a best friend who was married, considering his circumstances with his wife. At least that was what he told me. I always said, "There is always two sides to a story." But I never got her side of the story, not that I was expecting to, and it really did not matter because we were just best friends.

One day he asked, "Who am I to you?"

I said, "My friend."

My answer was slow, and I was unsure what he would say next. "My best friend," I repeated (with reservation). He was offended, but I could not understand why. So, I said to him, "Why are you offended?"

"I thought we were more than friends," he replied.

"This is why I said best friend. How could we be more than best friends?" I asked, confused. "Because of your circumstance (you are married) we cannot be more than best friends."

This was when our friendship shifted and not for the worst. Our friendship became closer. I realized he had begun to have deeper feelings for me, and I was amazed. Why? because I did not expect nor think that our friendship would go any deeper. However, it did, and we found ourselves telling each other, "I love you" just about every day. In the back of my mind, I thought, "How long is this going to last (rolling of the eyes)?"

Needless to say, I continued to go with the flow and BAM. We were wondering how we got to that place. Not long after that, our friendship of many years came to a halt (a screeching halt). That was the worst feeling ever because many times I knew, without a doubt, God was speaking to the both of us. Also, he was showing me signs to slow things down, but there I was again, saying to the Lord, "We are best friends, and there is nothing wrong with me helping his state of mind when it came to his marriage, health, or just his well-being." It was a joy to feel as if I were helping with the process of healing someone, I thought. As young as I could remember, I was always drawn to helping people and fixing situations and circumstances, whether it was their health, addictions, or other things but not to this capacity.

A person who was very close to my heart (who I knew in high school) once told me, "You cannot always help people, especially the ones that do not want to be helped. You are not God.... You have to let God be God. He knows exactly what to do!"

"Even if we feel guilty, God is greater than our feelings, and he knows everything." (1 John 3:20 NLT New Living Translation)

It hurt when he said that to me, but I knew it was true. It was true then, and it still holds truth today. At the end of the day, I have NO REGRETS. In all of this, I learned that it was me who needed fixing as well...Lesson learned. When the spirit of God tells you to release or slow down in a relationship, situation, or in any circumstances, OBEY. "A blessing, if ye obey the commandments of the Lord your God, which I command you this day." (Deuteronomy 11:27 KJV King James Version)

At that point, I knew my best friend was emotionally and physically gone. However, two weeks prior to this, my best friend and I had begun playing a game called Tag through text with Bible scriptures and praise and worship songs. Wow, right. God already knew what was about to take place. HE knows All.

CHAPTER 2

STAT... THE UNEXPECTED

Early Saturday morning of June 16, 2016, I was showering, preparing for a Single's Symposium at my church. I began slipping down slowly in the tub and uncontrollably feeling lightheaded. Instantly, I began to pray, "Lord, please do not let me hit my head." I felt a slight headache. I thought…Oh Lord, what is happening to me? My arms and legs began to shake as I hung slightly over the side of the tub with just enough strength to hold my head upward. After about three minutes or so, the shaking stopped. As I lay there very weak and unable to move, I called out for my daughter, Kayla, in a very weak voice. She was asleep with her room door closed, so there was no response. I called out again a little louder and stronger, "Kayla." Still, no response. And again, with no response. The fourth time, I said, "Lord, please give me strength to call my daughter. This time, let her hear me. I called her again from deep down in my soul. It was a piercing sound and crystal clear. She came into the bathroom and said, "What's wrong, Mommy? what happened?"

I could only say, "My head." As I lay in the tub with my arms hanging over it as the warm, steaming water hit my body. I was trying to keep from hitting my head ---I felt dizzy.

Kayla then asked, "Should I call Aunt Jakki?"

I told her to wait a minute as I gathered my thoughts. She began pacing back and forth, from the bathroom to the hallway area. I said, "Kayla, just stand here." I felt as if I were gaining strength by looking at her. We were quiet for a moment. Then, I could only say, "Jesus, help me. Give me strength to get up!" Immediately I felt my body strengthening. I said repeatedly, "Jesus, Jesus, Jesus," as I lifted my body up and out of the tub. I walked slowly to my living room and began praying in my heavenly language for about 5 minutes.

Kayla said, "Mommy, please sit down."

I said, "NO, (shaking my head) not yet."

I knew the enemy was trying to take me out. I continued to pray in my heavenly prayer language. Suddenly, I heard and felt a sound of wind come over me, like a blanket...woosh! There was a sense of peace that followed. I knew then it was the presence of God. "And the peace of God, which passeth all understanding, shall keep your hearts and minds through Christ Jesus." (Philippians.4:7, King James Version) Then, I sat down on the sofa. I heard a soft gentle voice say, "Go be seen," which I knew was the gift of knowledge operating at that time. "But the wisdom from above is first of all pure. It is also peace loving, gentle at all times, and willing to yield to others. It is full of mercy and fruit of good deeds. It shows no favoritism and is always sincere." (James 3:17, NLT New Living Translation)

At that point, Kayla was on the phone talking with my sister and telling her I was going to the hospital. After she got off the phone, I told her to call 911 and get my robe, so I could have something on before they came. Yes, all this time I was praying in the nude. Within 5 minutes, the paramedics arrived. The paramedics took my vital signs and said, "Your blood pressure is extremely high, through the roof, 160/180. You need to go to the emergency room now." I agreed and told Kayla I needed some lotion. One of the paramedics named Joe (not his real name) said, "Really, lotion?"

I said, "I'm ashy, I just got out of the shower." He chuckled and said, Okay, Kayla, get your mom some lotion quickly."

They took me down the stairs on a stair chair. The whole way down, I said to the paramedics, "Please do not drop me."

They said, "We promise we will not drop you."

If they had dropped me, my life would have been over! Then, I started giving instructions to Kayla, "No speeding and take your time, I am going to Mary Immaculate Hospital (which was my employer for almost 20 years)."

As I was being transferred from the stair chair to the stretcher into the ambulance, I asked Joe if he could sit with me in the back. I felt a little anxiety kicking in.

He said, "We are not allowed to sit in the back with patients, but yes, I will sit in the back with you." Peter (the other paramedic, which is not his real name) was driving.

I could hear the radio redirecting us to Riverside Hospital and I said to Joe, "NO! Do not let him take me to Riverside Hospital. Please take me to Mary Immaculate where my family (coworkers) are, who I spent almost 20 years of my life with, please."

Joe told Peter sharply, "I do not care what the radio said. Take her to Mary Immaculate Hospital and hurry."

When I arrived at Mary Immaculate's Hospital Emergency Department, the nurses and doctors were walking really fast toward me saying, "Sharon, what happened? What is going on?"

I told them I had a real bad headache. Then, I heard someone say, "Get her to CT scan ...STAT... let us MOVE!"

At this point I was drifting in and out of consciousness. I was not aware of being in the CT scan room. Sometime later, I was conscious and back in the Emergency Department room. The doctor said, Sharon, you are hemorrhaging in your brain, and we have to get you out of here." Someone call transportation STAT, not the ambulance.... Nightgale - helicopter, and have her airlift to Bon Secours Depaul Medical Neurovascular Center in Norfolk, Virginia," he stated. The distance where I was being taken was about a 30 minutes' drive in a vehicle, depending on traffic, it could have been longer. "We must get her out of here STAT!" the doctor continued.

At this point, Kayla broke down into tears. I felt this heaviness come over me, and my eyes were filling with tears. Suddenly, I heard the soft gentle voice again say, Don't cry. Stay calm. Again, a sense of peace came over me, and I told Kayla, "Stop crying. I am going to be fine... I am going to be okay. Just be safe driving. Get directions to Bon Secours Depaul Medical Center and take your time."

As I was going in and out of consciousness, I could feel the wind from the helicopter as I was being transported. I had to be transferred because of the acuity of what was happening. By the time I arrived at

Bon Secours Depaul Medical Neurovascular Center, I was unconscious.

Additional images were taken to confirmed that I indeed had a Subarachnoid hemorrhage (SAH) and no additional bleeding occurred while in route to the treatment facility.

Figure 1- Subarachnoid Hemorrhage

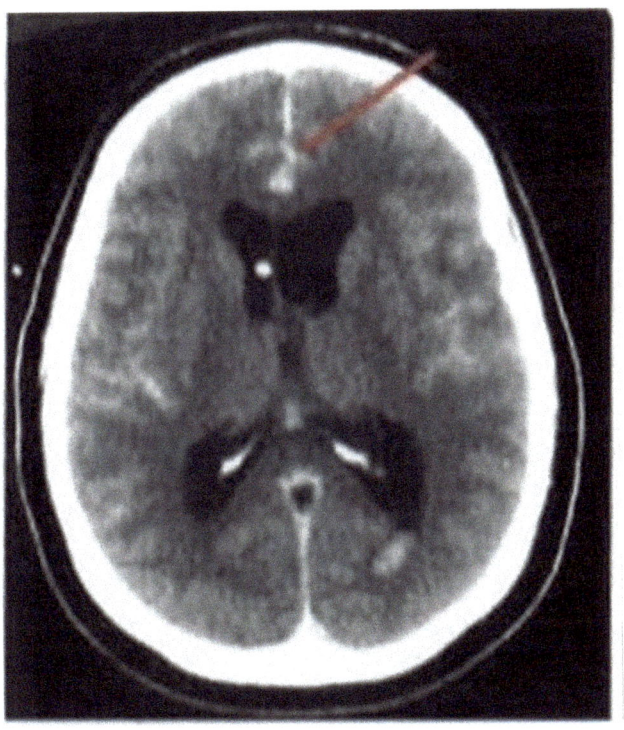

A SAH is known as a hemorrhagic stroke. Subarachnoid hemorrhage is a medical emergency that occurs from bulging blood vessels that ruptured within the brain, causing bleeding. This causes intracranial pressure to elevate, and if not promptly treated, it can lead to permanent brain damage or death.

A right frontal external ventricular drain (EVD) was placed which is a temporary method to relieve increased intracranial pressure caused by excess blood product from the SAH.

Figure 2- EVD Placement

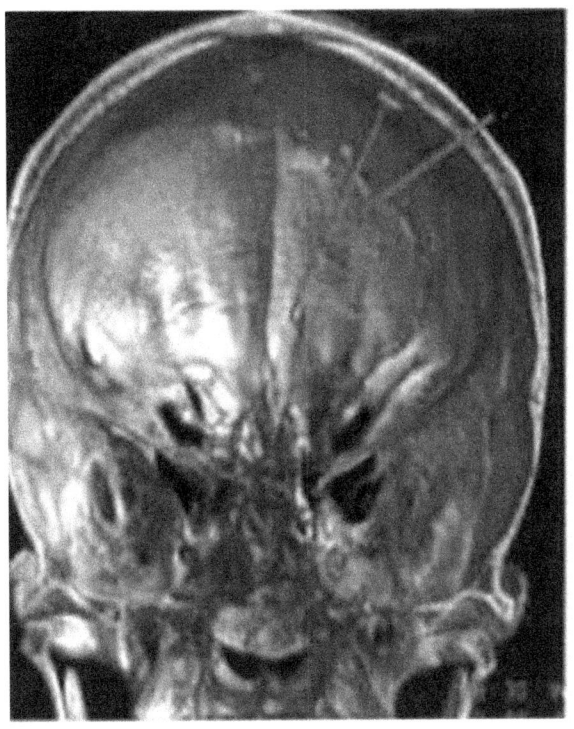

After the EVD (Figure 2) was placed emergently and the bleeding source secured. The bleeding source was identified as a ruptured distal left anterior cerebral artery aneurysm. A cerebral aneurysm is a bulging weakened area in the wall of an artery or multiple arteries in the brain resulting in an abnormal widening, ballooning, or bleb. The most common cause of an aneurysm(s) to rupture is uncontrolled high blood pressure. There are other causes for an aneurysm to rupture such as heavy lifting, straining, and STRESS.

After the increased intracranial pressure was treated, it was time to secure the bleeding source. The aneurysm was secured by the endovascular coiling method. The coiling method was performed by passing a catheter through the groin to secure the affected artery containing the aneurysm. Platinum coils were released and meshed into a ball within the aneurysm with hope of filling in the aneurysm to prevent blood pooling and additional weakening of the vessel causing re-ruptured bleeding.

Figure 3- Pre Coiling

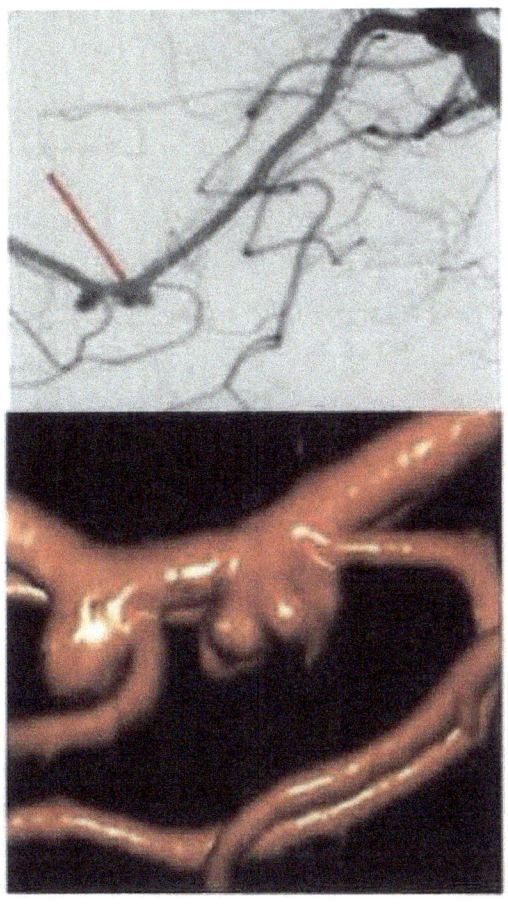

After about a 9-hour or more surgery, I slipped into a coma for a short period of time, and when I became conscious, there stood my cousin Valerie. I said, "Val," which is what I call her for short. I looked around at my surroundings. At that point, I knew I was in the hospital, and I came to the realization that I was in my right mind. "Thou wilt keep him in perfect peace, whose mind is stayed on thee: because he trusteth in thee. Trust ye in the Lord forever: for in the Lord, Jehovah, is everlasting strength." (Isaiah 26: 3-4 KJV) I then had many members of my family, close friends, and my daughters' father, Kelvin, stop by later that day as well. At this time, only two at a time could visit me. I spoke to them calling them by their names. They were standing in amazement! Shortly after everyone left, the nurses were in and out of my room checking my vitals. One of the nurses stood at my bedside and said to me, (as she was tearing up and trembling in her voice), "Sharon, I know we are not supposed to show our emotions about our patients to the patient, but you were very sick, and we thought you were not going to make it, and I know that there is a higher power, and HE is definitely looking over you!" "And if I be lifted up from the earth, will draw all men unto me." (John 12:32 KJV)

I said, "Yes, do not cry...there is a higher power, and HIS name is Jesus, and HE loves me, and I am okay now. HE'S GOT ME!"

The next day when my best friend (BF) was told I was in the hospital, he came and stood by my side holding my hand. As we gazed into each other eyes, we both were speechless, not knowing this would be his one and only visit…

CHAPTER 3

RECOVERY

A couple of weeks went by. Then, my sister came to visit me, I said, "Jakki, give me a mirror, I want to see what I look like." She handed me a mirror. As I stared at the tube in my head, the tears began rolling down my face. I thought, look at what God has brought me through and how much He really loves me! I lay confined to the bed with the tube in my head used to drain the blood from where I was hemorrhaging. I was only able to lift my head 6-12 inches.

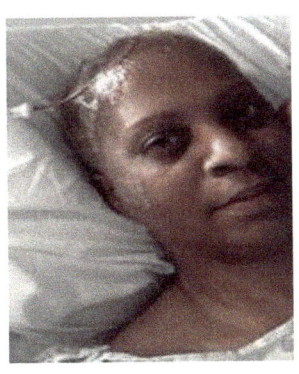

All kinds of thoughts were going through my mind. How long will I be here? How long will I be confined to this bed? Will I be able to go back to work? When will I be able to drink water? Yes, water. I am a water drinker, and I usually drink water all day, every day. However, doctors ordered that I drink no water. The closest to water I could drink was Gatorade because the water could have caused swelling on my brain. My sodium levels of chemistry drawl would have been off, and it would have caused the reduction of other levels. During day six of my hospitalization, I underwent treatment of vasospasm with intraarterial vasodilator.

This treatment minimized the impact of aneurysmal subarachnoid hemorrhage-induced cerebral vasospasm refractory to standard management. However, the worse part of this trauma was not over.

As the night approached, I began to experience legs spasms because of inflammation of the nerves and being confined to bed at this time. This happened every night for about a week or two with my sister by my bedside. If she was not by my bed side, she was on the phone with me as I cried, moaned and groaned, calling out the name of Jesus. I continued to quote the scripture, "I shall not die, but live, and declare the works of the Lord." (Psalms 118:17 KJV)

I could remember saying to my sister, "I can't. I can't. I can't." She asked me, "You can't what?" And I could never finish the sentence. However, my thought was, I cannot bear this pain any longer. But I felt if I had finished that sentence, I would have been giving into the pain and giving up completely. During the night, the pain was the worst. One of the LPN's named Soja (not her real name) came into my room to check on me as I moaned and groaned. She said, "Oh, you cannot be hurting that bad. You are NOT hurting that bad! It took everything in me not to say anything to her, but I really wanted to cuss her out. You better believe I reported her to the nurse manager that was on duty that night. I let her know that when Soja was on duty again, she was NOT to come in my room because I would not tolerate negativity! I wanted positive vibes only in my room! As a few days went by... Guess what!? She did not return to my room; she would peek in every now and then, but she dared not to enter. As a few more days went by, she entered my room with apologies and positive vibes. I accepted her apology.

From that point on, she entered my room with positive vibes only.

However, Kelvin came on a regular basis to visit me.

I believe this is the perfect time to give you a little history about Kelvin and I. Sabrina, a friend of both of ours, would always say, "I have someone I need for you to meet, and I think you both would like each other." She introduced us the summer of our tenth-grade year, and we exchanged phone numbers. After the meet and greet, Sabrina and I drove off.

A few days went by, I had not heard from him. One day Sabrina and I decided to walk to the school where he played outdoor basketball, not knowing if he would be there, to my surprise he was there. He came over to me and we talked for a short time. Then he went back to playing basketball. As she and I was walking away, I clearly heard this voice say, "That is your husband." When I heard this, I knew it was the Lord. I immediately started laughing and stopped walking. I said to Sabrina, "I just heard the Lord say, "that is my husband."

She said, "Wow, I knew I was supposed to introduce you guys." Not too long after a few late telephone conversations, we were in an exclusive relationship. Kelvin and I dated throughout high school, and he became my true love. A year after high school, he enlisted in the military, stationed in Germany. He asked me to marry him before leaving, and out of fear I let the person I knew was to be my husband go without me. I could not bear the thought of leaving my father and mother, so the separation sat in.

One day Kelvin came to visit and noticed I was not eating much at all. He said, "You must eat if you want to get out of here. He then picked up the fork and began feeding me saying, "You must eat in order to gain your strength." I began eating.

After a couple of days had gone by, I noticed he had stopped coming to visit me. When I spoke with Kayla later that day I asked, "Have you seen or heard from your dad.

She replied, "Yes what is wrong?

I said, "I have not seen him in a couple of days. Call him to see if he is alright," and she did. His response was that he did not want to interfere with me and my friend (BF). It was obvious that they had met each other at some point. I told her to tell him he better get over here and see me! Needless to say, he came back visiting me on a regular basis. I told him he was always welcome to come to see me. "If I had to give a reason why, you are the father of our children.

"On June 24th, I underwent EVD removal. Surviving such an ordeal was not quite over as follow-up studies were recommended and residual deficits of the hemorrhagic stroke remained. Many more diagnostic and follow-up procedures were performed to determine if any additional procedures that involved treatment would be needed.

At the time of initially treating the ruptured aneurysm mentioned earlier there were three others identified at that time. The follow up study known as cerebral angiogram (CA) was performed on August 3rd. The procedure determined if additional treatment was needed to be performed to the previously treated ruptured cerebral aneurysm. On February 8th, a flow diversion of the left anterior cerebral aneurysms was performed. The flow diverter treated two aneurysms on the same vessel at once, which at the time considered the new improved treatment for multiple irregular aneurysms on the same artery.

Figure 4-Post Coiling

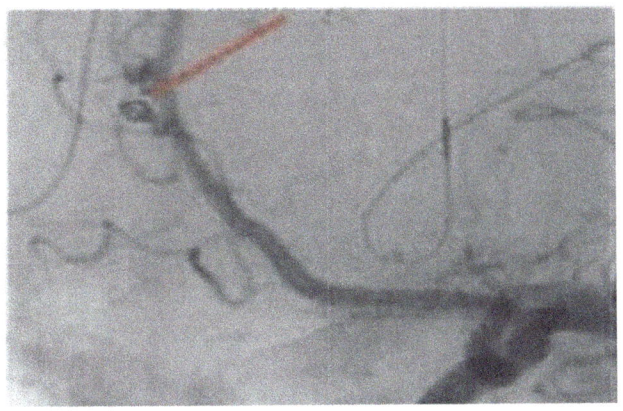

Continued surveillances were being performed to assess for limited flow through the diverter by undergoing cerebral angiogram initially six months post procedure on August 22, 2017; then it was performed again six months later on March 13, 2018, and the most recent on April 25,2019. As time goes by and the stability of the diverter is maintained, the length of time in between follow-up assessments will increase and become longer in intervals, and post procedure risk of complication will decrease.

Figure 5-Post flow diverter

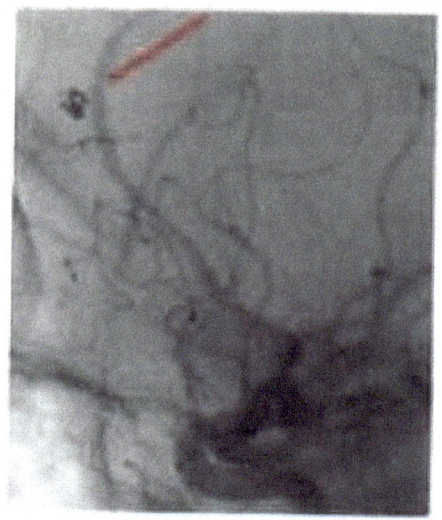

Figure 6-Post flow diverter

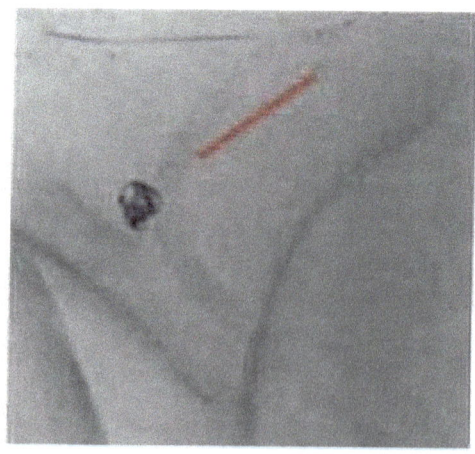

I continued to get better and was discharged from the hospital on June 27, 2016, directly to Riverside Rehabilitation Center. Upon my arrival, I was still a little weak, had some anxieties going on, and some back and leg pain. However, as I lay in bed, I took the time to reflect on how this was all working in my favor from the beginning. Kayla was home when it all started. Therefore, I had someone with me. Kaiya was with her cousins for the day. Mary Immaculate emergency department nurses, technicians, and doctors met me at the door, and it did not appear that it was busy that morning. Dr. John Baker, one of the greatest Neuroendovascular interventionist in the country, was available for me. It appeared everyone was in the right place at the right time to care for me. I am SO grateful!!

As the days went by, I continued to feel better physically with all the exercises that was assigned for me to do. They were amazed at my speedy progress. I was quickly improving, but emotionally I felt I was slipping into depression. I was at a dark place, literally... spiritually and mentally. I would say to myself, "I am NOT supposed to be here. Lord, you must get me out of here. Show me what to do and when to do it, so this process will not be long."

I was confined to a wheelchair, at the time my legs still were not strong enough for me to walk without assistance. I had to participate in several group talking sessions as one of my cognitive assignments. As I looked around me, people were worse off than me, which made me feel so sad. I was feeling, I do not belong here, and I knew I was not going to be there long, and I had to work harder with my progress of getting better. The next day, I was doing my physical assignments. I thought to myself, "The Fourth of July weekend is quickly approaching, and I will not be here during that time. I must work harder!" And I did. My estimated length of stay at the rehabilitation center was 10 days. However, the healing progress I made was nothing less than a miracle, and I was discharged on July 2, 2016. Yes, that is right.... discharged in 5 days, a couple of days before the Fourth of July! TO GOD BE THE GLORY. "Now unto him that is able to do exceedingly abundantly above all that we ask or think, according to the power that worketh in us." (Ephesians 3:20 KJV) I was discharged home with Kayla and Kelvin.

After being released from the rehabilitation center, Kelvin stayed with us for a limited time caring for us.

He made sure I had my medicines, ate properly, and anything else that I may have needed. Also, he made sure that our girls were up and off to school on time. However, after a couple of weeks, I was ready for him to go home so I could get back close to my normal life as possible, keeping everything under control.

I followed up with my neurosurgeon Dr. John Baker periodically for a CTA (Computed Tomography Angiography) and a DSA (Digital Subtraction Angiography).

CHAPTER 4

NEW LIFE

Nevertheless, a shift happened. As soon as I thought Kelvin was going to leave, we began to become closer in our relationship. When he felt comfortable enough to go home, it was only for a short period of time. We started to discuss our living arrangements.

Keep in mind I was not working, and no income was coming in for me at this time. My mother took care of ALL my needs and wants! This was such a blessing to have a mother be able to do such a thing for her child. I was and still am so grateful!! As Kelvin and I discussed our living arrangements, he suggested he leave his home and come live with me to take on all my bills, rather than paying bills at both homes. I gave it a long thought and prayed because I have always said, "I would not live with anyone before marriage."

One evening, Kelvin and I went out for dinner. To his surprise, I told him I agreed with his suggestion to move in with me. He was speechless, shocked, and happy all at the same time. This was relieving my mother of all that she had done and was still doing for me. I thought, *WOW*...I hesitated. I was scared, unsure, and so many thoughts were going through my mind. *We are not married, are we even thinking about marriage at this point in our lives?* All of these love emotions started to surface that I thought were dead and gone! He moved in, and it was uphill from there. We got engaged in April 2018 and went to pre-marital counseling. At our last pre-marital counseling session, I thought this was profound......Kelvin was asked,

"What is stopping you from getting married now? Is it money?"

Kelvin said, "Yes because she wants a wedding." He was then asked another question. "What is stopping you from setting a wedding date now?" To my surprise, he said nothing. Pastor E and Kelvin set the wedding date, and I agreed.

We decided to do it God's way, and we were married on October 20, 2018, and we had the most beautiful wedding and reception on August 17, 2019. Now, here we are as Mr. and Mrs. Kelvin Jones. We definitely got a thing going on, and the journey continues…

Here you will find unexpected undertaking experiences from a few of my family members that I had an opportunity to interview:

"I did not know if my mom was going to make it through this or not. I felt weak each time I tried to go into her hospital room. Finally, I got enough strength to go in, and I cried. I could not bear to see my mom like that, but deep down inside I knew she was going to make it." Kaiya (My daughter)

"My mom asked for lotion for her feet at such a time as this. She is funny. That still cracks me up every time I think about that because that was such an important and most frightening time of her life. She demanded that I grab some lotion for her ashy feet before leaving for the hospital. Through it all, I would hear my mom saying, "I am going to be okay; all things are

possible through Christ who strengthens me." I felt weak in my knees, devastated and frightened! However, I pulled myself together and remained strong no matter what." Kayla (My daughter)

"I was out of the area when I received the news that my daughter's mom was hospitalized, and immediately I traveled back to my daughters. When I arrived, I went straight in the hospital. I was numb and speechless, thinking this should have been me and not her." Kelvin (My love)

"I was in disbelief. I had just seen her the day before. I told the family, "Sharon has been hospitalized and do not ask questions…PRAY!" Also, I had to tell Kaiya. OMG, I was not sure how she would respond. When I did tell her, it was as if she was in shock.

"When I walked into the hospital room and asked Sharon, who was I, she said, ACE I smiled. I already knew she was going to pull through." Valerie (My Cousin)

"After all I had gone through physically, emotionally, and mentally, my spirit was still alert. I heard a song playing "Let the Peace of God Reign." I did not realize where it was playing from. As I looked around, I soon realized it was playing from my phone that was in my pocket. That gave me peace."

As I looked to the sky, a swarm of birds were flying, the wind shifted and the trees swaying back and forth, a scripture came to my mind, Psalm 150:6 "Let everything that hath breath Praise the LORD." (Psalm 150:6 KJV)

When the doctor said to me, "Only one out of ten people usually make it out of this."

I kindly replied, "This one will make it. I am not worried about that." It was because he was the top doctor in the country, and he was performing the surgery.

Amazingly after the surgery, and I was able to see her, she said, "Hey, Jakki," as if nothing never happened.

I said, "Look at God. It was nobody but God."

Jakki (My one and only sister)

ABOUT THE AUTHOR

Sharon D. Jones was born in Newport News, Virginia but raised in Hampton, Virginia. She is the wife of her forever longtime love, Kelvin Jones. Sharon has two daughters and two grandchildren.

She enjoys traveling, music, dancing, skating, spending time with her family and encouraging people to move from the pain to their purpose in life. She is a Prayer Leader at the church she attends.

Since writing this book, she believes more than ever that the Lord has given her the anointing through prayer to break the chains of bondage, spiritually, physically, and emotionally and to set God's people free.

His Glory Creations Publishing, LLC is an International Christian Book Publishing Company, established in 2017, which helps launch the creative fiction and non-fiction works of new, aspiring, and seasoned authors across the globe, through stories that are inspirational, empowering, life changing or educational in nature, including anthologies, poetry, journals, children's books, and audio books.

DESIRE TO KNOW MORE?

Contact Information:
CEO/Founder: Felicia C. Lucas

www.hisglorycreationspublishing.com
Email: hgcpublishingllc@gmail.com
Office Phone: 919-679-1706

Facebook: His Glory Creations Publishing
Instagram: His Glory Creations Publishing
YouTube: His Glory Creations Publishing

www.ingramcontent.com/pod-product-compliance
Lightning Source LLC
Chambersburg PA
CBHW061805070526
44586CB00023B/2726